Narcissus:
The Man, The Myth, The Flower

A poem on the 12 links of dependent arising

Steve Price

To the causes and conditions that have made you, me and all things possible.

INTRODUCTION

The 12 links of dependent arising were taught by Buddha to help us see the process by which we suffer more than we need to.

Everything, including each of us, is momentary, dependent on causes and conditions that are constantly changing. When we fail to see this, we tend to view and treat the world according to our own personal mythologies.

As a result, we think, speak, do and label without seeing the consequences; use our attention and senses haphazardly; crave what we think we want; grab what we think will make us happy; and then think we're "reinventing ourselves" when really we're just going through the same old patterns with a new spouse, career, or, if you believe in rebirth, body. Once we see the cycle, we can begin to interrupt it.

Selflessness and wisdom go hand in hand. To consider the well being of others is just plain sane. If we can see our narcissism as a painful but effective reminder to be kind, it can be a beautiful thing.

1. Self-Centered View

Little Narcissus
Looks out the window
And sees his reflection.
Everything beyond—
Trees, clouds,
People in the park—
Are insignificant.
This is framed
Like a painting
Of reality.

Tiresias, a man made wise
From spending
Seven years as a woman
And having his eyesight
Replaced with foresight,
Tells Liriope:
That spoiled brat of yours
Might live to a ripe old age
Provided he never sees
He's just a myth.

2. Impressions Left By Self-Centered Thoughts, Words And Actions

Narcissus, hunting stags,
Hears footsteps.
Who's there? says he.
Who's there? says Echo.
He thinks:
She's mocking me!
He can't see
She loves him
And just lacks the words.
The best she can do
Is repeat his.
When she puts her arms
Around his neck
He pushes her
Deep into the woods
To wither and die.
But her voice
Keeps echoing
In him.

3. Attention Wandering At Whim

Narcissus runs
From Echo's reverberations,
Sidestepping hearts
Of other admirers
He'd discarded.
His mind is a drunken
Monkey staggering
From tree to
Deer carcass to chirp
To neck twinge to
Scent of rotting log…
Nothing of use to him.
He has his legs
Take him to Tiresias.

**4. Things That Seem Important
And Names To Make Them Seem More So**

You're made,
Says Tiresias,
Of your own doings
Using that body
Of earth and water,
Fire for digestion,
Air to breathe,
Feelings for, against,
Or utter disregard
And greedy senses
To hunt things,
Twist them into ideas
And name them the way
Your parents named you.
You've shoved
Everyone away
And all that shoving
Shoved you here.

Narcissus snores.
He's using the man's monotone
As a sedative.

When he wakes up
Tiresias asks him:
Would you mind
If I name a disorder after you?
Narcissus is flattered.

5. Self-Centered Senses

Narcissus' body
Came with two eyes,
Two ears, a nose, tongue,
Nerves, and a brain,
Equipping Narcissus
To revolve the world
Around Narcissus.
He uses his senses
As arrows,
Hunting whatever
His self-absorbed self
Can absorb.

And now a guy
Narcissus belittled
And gave a sword
To kill himself
Yells to the sky:
Let that pompous ass
Fall in love with himself
And right into hell!
When Nemesis hears this
She makes Narcissus
His own nemesis.

6. Contact!

Thirst draws Narcissus
To clear water
Undisturbed by shepherds,
Goats, or even a branch
From the trees
Blocking the sun for him.
He lies on his belly
And what he sees sets him
Ablaze with desire:
Ivory neck,
Stars for eyes,
Cheeks like roses crushed in snow,
Locks soft enough for Apollo.
His dry lips meet the wet.

7. The Feeling

Narcissus fizzes
Like a cloud on fire.
His brain melts.
His blood cools
And at the same time boils,
Steaming from
His skin and hair.
He evaporates
Into the feeling

But then
The feeling is gone,
Leaving only his thirst
Burning worse than ever.
His throat crackles.

8. Craving

Narcissus' eyes,
Riveted to the water,
Are parched from not blinking.
He dares not drink
And disrupt his reflection.
He rasps:

When I smile, he smiles.
When I weep, he weeps.
When I speak, his lips
Form my words.
Finally, someone
Who understands me!
Tell me, old man,
Am I in love or hell?
Or are they the same?

You're afraid, replies Tiresias,
He'll reject you
As you've rejected others.

Have some bread, says Ceres,
Who made it herself.

How do you expect me
To swallow that? Narcissus croaks.
I'm out of saliva.

Rest, soothes Tiresias.
Take a nap.

Leave us be!
Narcissus hisses.
When he turns to glare at them
They aren't there
And never were.
He's been alone all along.
He looks in the water,
Sees it's just a reflection,
That he's fallen in love with himself,
A self he's made up
As he's made up everyone else.
And yet he burns for more
But of what he doesn't know.

9. Grabbing What Can't Last

Narcissus
Clings to his view
Of being all-powerful
While having
No power at all.
All his bowing
To his reflection
Has given him whiplash.
All his praying
To leave his body
Has kept him in it.
He's grasping
For anything permanent
Or painless or anything
But everything slips
Like flames through his fingers.

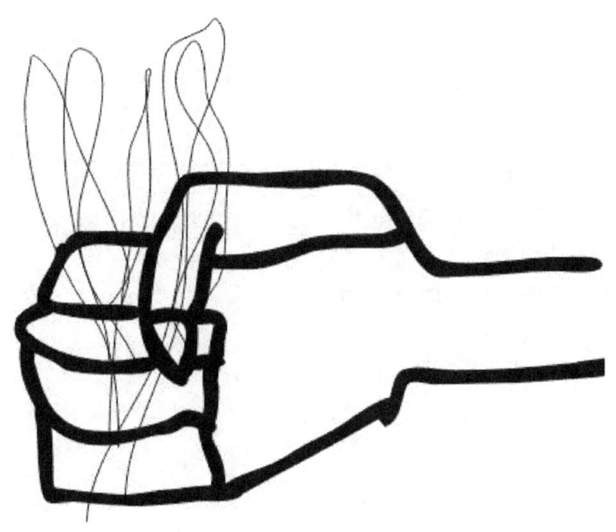

10. Developing Into Something Else

It's night,
Too dark to see his reflection.
The black water
Is now a river in hell.
Farewell, he sighs.
Farewell, sighs Echo.
His identity crisis
Is complete.
It's a dark enlightenment.
There's no Narcissus,
Just a name
Derived from *narke*,
The root of *narcotic*,
Inducing numbness, sleep, dormancy,
A bulb frozen in the ground
For months of cold incubation.

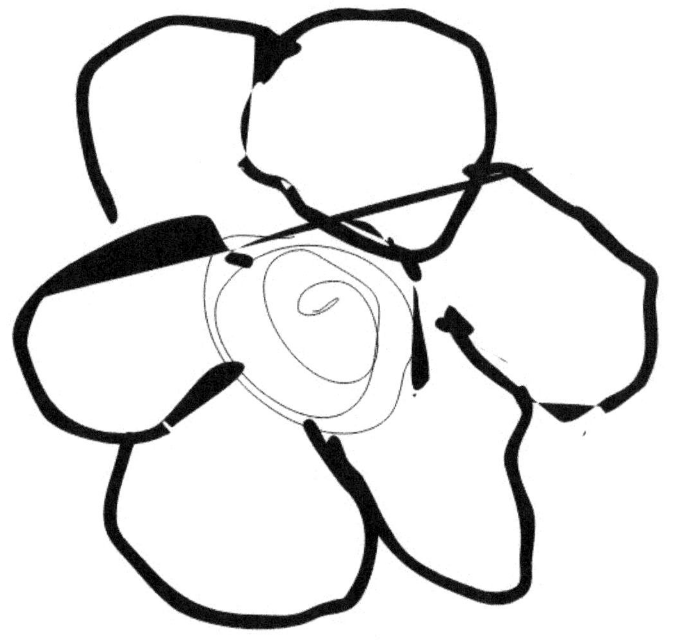

11. New Life

Spring sun
Penetrates the soil.
Roots descend, stem rises.
Narcissus poeticus blooms,
A white, yellow-hearted trumpet,
Mute and alone.

12. Old Age And Death

Narcissus died young,
Avoiding the pain of aging
And passing it along in another form.
All the maidens from the water
And the trees are grieving,
Mean as he was.
Their sobs come back to them,
Returned by Echo.

They prepare the pyre
But when they come for the body,
It's gone, already burned
Away by desire
And replaced with a flower.
If put in a vase
With other kinds,
A sap would bleed
From the stem
And poison them.

Look beyond yourself.
See beauty
Even in those who can't.
See the world
Not how you want it to be
But as it is.
See that your life
And all that you are
Depends on everything
And everyone you're not.

OTHER BOOKS BY STEVE PRICE

Crab Apples: Stories & Poems
Brake Light
They Don't Have A Word For It
John Doe's Diamond
Arrows of Love: A New Version of The Bhagavad Gita
A Bowler's View of the Tao Te Ching
Crawling Back To Patanjali
Assembly Instructions for Your Head
Writing From Scratch
How's Your Ice Cream?
Swami On Call
Coping With Bliss
Song of the Heart With No Walls
Clam In The Sky
Rocky (with Olive Price)
Can I Have One Moment of Peace?
Journal of Lovesickness, Vol. 11

To learn more, visit onemomentofpeace.org.

www.ingramcontent.com/pod-product-compliance
Lightning Source LLC
Chambersburg PA
CBHW051941150726

47999CB00006B/2312